Summer on the farm

by Jillian Powell

an imprint of Hodder Children's Books

Titles in the series

Summer on the farm
Autumn on the farm
Winter on the farm
Spring on the farm

Picture Acknowledgements
The publishers would like to thank the following for allowing their photographs to be reproduced in this book: Cephas 19 (Frank B. Higham bottom); Bruce Coleman Ltd 5 (Eric Crichton top), (J. Murray bottom), 8, 19 (Hans Reinhard top), 11 (N. McAllister), 24 (Jeremy Grayson), 29 (Jane Burton top); Frank Lane Picture Agency 18 (P. Dean), 28 (Ray F. Bird bottom); Francesca Motisi 12, 13, *back cover*; Natural History Photographic Agency *title page*, 8 (G. Gainsburgh bottom), 6 (bottom), 7, 15 (both), 17 (David Woodfall), 9 (bottom), 25 (both), 29 (G.I. Bernard), 10 (inset), 26 (bottom), 27 (bottom) E.A. Janes, 16 (Matt Bain), 20, 21 (bottom), 22 (top) Laurie Campbell, 21 (top) David Tomlinson, 26 (top) Martin Wender, 27 (top) Joe Blossom; Oxford Scientific Films Ltd *front cover* (Ronald Toms), 9 (Niall Benvie top); Farmer's Weekly Picture Library 4 (Roger G. Howard), 6 (top), 10 (main) 14 (Raymond Lea); Wayland Picture Library 22 (bottom), 23, 30, 31.

Series editor: Francesca Motisi
Book editor: Joan Walters
Series and book designer: Jean Wheeler

First published in 1996 by
Wayland (Publishers) Limited
This paperback edition published in 2001 by Hodder Wayland,
an imprint of Hodder Children's Books

© Hodder Wayland 1996

British Cataloguing in Publication Data
Powell, Jillian
Summer on the farm. - (The Farming Year)
1. Agriculture - Juvenile literature
2. Summer - Juvenile literature
I. Title II. Series
630

ISBN 0-7502-3435-0

Typeset by Jean Wheeler
Printed and bound by G. Canale and C.S.p.A., Turin, Italy

Contents

Introduction 4
Spraying and watering crops 6
The soft fruit harvest 8
The vegetable harvest 10
The combine harvester and baler 12
Haymaking 14
Silage making 16
Dairy and beef farming 18
The deer farm 20
The trout farm 22
Sheep farming 24
Indoor and outdoor farming 26
Summer events 28
The farming year calendar 30
Glossary 32
Books to read 32
Index 32

Introduction

Summer is a busy time on the farm. The days are long and the weather may be hot and sunny. Sunshine ripens crops and you can tell when they are ready for harvest because they change colour. Wheat and barley turn from green to golden yellow.

Summer fruits such as redcurrants become ripe and red.

Summer is the time for the farmer to cut the grass to make hay, which is fed to farm animals in the winter.

Spraying and watering crops

In dry weather the farmer waters the crops using giant water sprinklers.

Farmers may spray their crops with chemicals to kill insects, diseases and weeds. Chemicals can be dangerous, so they must be used very carefully.

Organic farmers think it is better not to use chemicals. This field of wheat has not been sprayed. That is why poppies and other wild flowers are growing among the wheat.

The soft fruit harvest

Summer sunshine ripens soft fruits such as strawberries, gooseberries, raspberries and blackcurrants.

Soft fruit must be picked very carefully or it could get squashed and the farmer would not be able to sell it.

Some fruit is picked by hand but bigger fruit farms use machines. This raspberry harvester in Scotland gathers the fruits without squashing them.

On a pick-your-own farm you can pick your own fruit and pay for each basket when you have weighed it.

The vegetable harvest

In the early summer, the farmer starts harvesting potatoes. The potato harvester lifts whole plants out of the earth then gently pulls the potatoes away from the stems and leaves, without spoiling them.

On small farms, potatoes are dug out of the ground by hand.

Other vegetable crops, such as cauliflowers, beans and peas, also grow big enough to harvest in the summer.

After harvesting, the farmer may plough the fields and plant them with crops which can grow through the autumn and winter months, such as winter wheat, winter barley and oats.

The farmer may also plant vegetables such as parsnips and turnips.

The combine harvester and baler

When the wheat and barley crops are ripe, the farmer harvests them with a huge machine called a combine harvester.

A combine is like a giant mechanical monster, gobbling up the grains of wheat or barley. It cuts the stalks and picks up the grains. Then it spits out the stalks from the back of the machine and these are left behind as straw.

The grain is emptied from the combine into a trailer and taken back to the farm to be stored.

Another machine called a baler collects the straw. It makes square or round bundles called bales. The baler ties the bales with strong string then drops them back on the field.

Later, the bales will be carried back to the farm to be stored in a dry place.

Haymaking

In summer, farm animals can feed on the fresh grass, but the farmer must plan ahead for the winter when the grass will stop growing. Grass is made into hay to feed the animals in the winter.

Hay is grass which has been dried in the sun. The tractor pulls a mower which cuts the grass and leaves it in rows. Then the farmer fixes another tool to the tractor which picks up and turns over the grass to help it dry.

When the grass is quite dry, a baling machine sucks it up and spins it into bales.

The bales are loaded on to a trailer which takes them back to the farm to be stored.

Silage making

Making silage is a way of keeping grass as soft and juicy as possible after it has been cut. A machine called a forage harvester cuts and sucks up the grass.

The milking parlour must be kept very clean so germs cannot get into the milk. After milking is over, the parlour is washed down.

The milk is pumped into a big tank which keeps it cool. Once a day, a tanker arrives at the farm to collect the milk.

Spring calves

Some calves are born in the spring. A cow usually has her first calf when she is about two years old. On a farm where cattle are kept for beef, the calves feed on their mothers' milk. They wear tags in their ears so the farmer can watch how well they grow.

On a dairy farm, calves are fed on their mothers' milk for only a few days. Then the farmer feeds them on dried milk until they can eat hay, silage and fresh grass.

 The deer farm

Some farmers keep deer for their meat, which is called venison.

The deer may live indoors in the cold winter months and in the spring they come out to graze on fresh grass.

In the late spring, the female deer give birth to calves. The farmer weighs each calf and puts a tag in its ear. The calves drink their mothers' milk until they are old enough to graze on fresh grass.

The sheep farm

Spring is the time when most lambs are born. Female sheep are called ewes. Some farmers bring the ewes into sheds to have their lambs. The farmer feeds the ewes on hay and silage.

The lambs drink their mothers' milk which helps them grow strong and healthy.

As the weather gets warmer, the ewes can go outside to graze on fresh grass.

 The salmon farm

In spring, salmon which live wild in rivers swim out to sea. They stay in the sea for a year or more until they swim back to their home rivers to lay their eggs.

The salmon farmer copies nature. In spring, the farmer moves the young salmon from big tanks of water on the salmon farm to pens of seawater.

The salmon can swim around in the seawater inside huge nets ten metres deep. They grow for another year until they are big enough to eat.

The salmon farmer feeds them on fish food which has all the goodness they need.

The fruit farm

In spring, the trees on the fruit farm are covered with blossom. The trees can only make fruits if pollen is carried from one flower to another. This is called pollination.

The fruit farmer needs bees to pollinate the flowers. On a dry spring day a beekeeper visits the farm with hives of bees which are placed near the fruit trees.

The bees fly from flower to flower to gather sweet nectar which they will make into honey. As they visit each flower, pollen sticks to their legs and bodies.

When they visit the next flower, the pollen rubs off their bodies and sticks to the female part of the flower. This pollinates the flower so it can grow into a fruit.

Spring chicks

Spring is a time for birds to lay eggs. When a hen mates with a male bird, called a cockerel, she lays eggs that will hatch into chicks.

Hens that are kept indoors lay eggs all year round. The electric lighting makes them think that it is always springtime. The eggs are hatched in special machines which are kept as warm as a hen's body. After hatching, the chicks live and grow together in special conditions indoors.

This hen and her young are free-range chickens, which means they spend their days outside. They start having their chicks in the spring. Chicks remind us that spring is here, with all the new life the season brings.

The farming year calendar

Spring

Sowing crops for summer and autumn harvest
Harvesting vegetables grown through the winter
Fertilizing and spraying crops against weeds and diseases
Lambing
Putting animals out to graze
Silage making

Summer

Harvesting vegetables and soft fruits
Watering crops
Haymaking
Silage making
Sheep shearing and sheep dipping
Harvesting crops such as wheat and barley

Autumn

Ploughing fields after harvest
Sowing winter wheat and barley
Harvesting fruits such as apples and pears
Harvesting potatoes and sugar beet
Autumn calving
Hedge trimming

Winter

Clearing and draining ditches
Pruning fruit trees
Housing animals
Early indoor lambing
Fertilizing crops
Repairing farm buildings, fences and machinery

Glossary

Chemicals Sprays and powders used by farmers to keep their crops healthy.
Diseases Illnesses that can kill plants and animals.
Germs Tiny living things that can make us ill.
Harvested Crops that have been cut and gathered in.
Mates Joins together with another animal to have babies.
Milking parlour A farm building where cows are taken to be milked.
Nectar A sweet liquid made by flowers.
Plough To turn the earth over with a metal tool called a plough.
Pollen The yellow powdery grains made by flowers.
Silage Grass that has been cut and wrapped in black plastic to keep it juicy.
Tanker A truck with a big tank on the back for carrying liquids such as milk.
Udder The part of a female cow which holds her milk.

Books to read

Farming, Sue Hadden (Wayland, 1991)
Farming, Ruth Thomson (Watts, 1994)
Let's Visit a Farm series, Sarah Doughty and Diana Bentley (Wayland, 1989-90)

Index

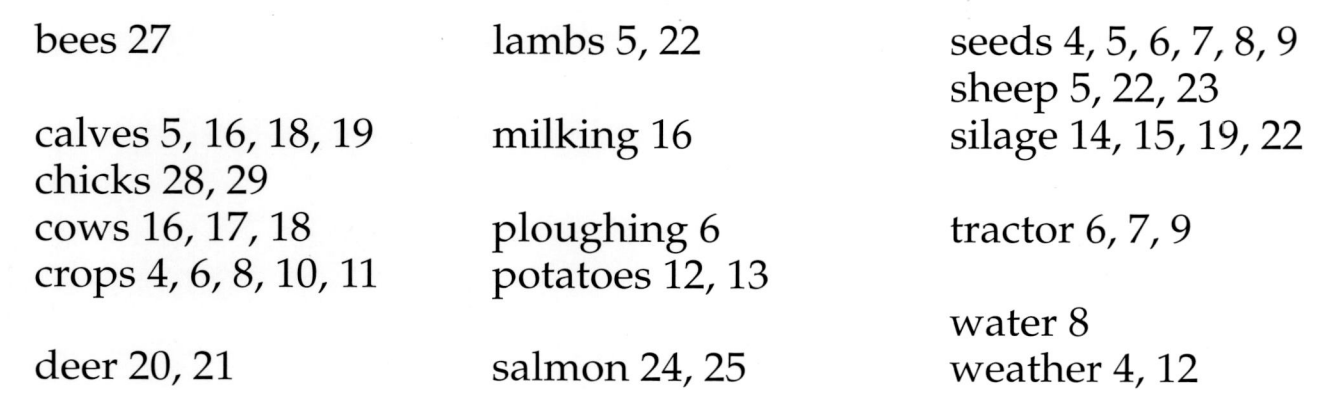

bees 27

calves 5, 16, 18, 19
chicks 28, 29
cows 16, 17, 18
crops 4, 6, 8, 10, 11

deer 20, 21

lambs 5, 22

milking 16

ploughing 6
potatoes 12, 13

salmon 24, 25

seeds 4, 5, 6, 7, 8, 9
sheep 5, 22, 23
silage 14, 15, 19, 22

tractor 6, 7, 9

water 8
weather 4, 12